I0006823

10 Minutes to Organized Internet Usage

10 Minutes to Organized Internet Usage

The Internet Companion

Tanya M. Griffin
&
Ginae B. McDonald

Writers Club Press
San Jose New York Lincoln Shanghai

10 Minutes to Organized Internet Usage
The Internet Companion

All Rights Reserved © 2001 by Tanya M. Griffin and Ginae B. McDonald

No part of this book may be reproduced or transmitted in any form or by any means, graphic, electronic, or mechanical, including photocopying, recording, taping, or by any information storage retrieval system, without the permission in writing from the publisher.

Writers Club Press
an imprint of iUniverse, Inc.

For information address:
iUniverse, Inc.
5220 S. 16th St., Suite 200
Lincoln, NE 68512
www.iuniverse.com

ISBN: 0-595-21428-2

Printed in the United States of America

Dedication

Lovingly dedicated to Tanya's parents, Mr. and Mrs. William A. Griffin, my mother, Nona B. McDonald and my sister, Sherlynn Nunn. We are grateful for their support and presence in our lives.

CONTENTS

PREFACE

When you very first picked up this book, I'm guessing that you knew what this book was for. I'm guessing that you were NOT looking for, "Toilet Painting for a More Profound Bathroom Experience." My thinking is that anyone who has sat for endless hours in front of the Internet, visiting web sites and checking e-mail KNOWS what it's like to go from one site to another, in need of a user identity and password that have been long forgotten or otherwise not recorded.

I've been using the Internet for the past eight years and during that time, the organization of passwords, user identities and e-mail addresses has always been an issue. Sometimes, I'd even avoid web sites that required a password and/or user identity, because I didn't have it together enough to keep that information without losing/forgetting it.

And just forget about favorite URL's! I can't count the number of times my hard drive has crashed, causing the loss (most of it permanent) of much data, to include favorite URL's.

After seven years, I learned to record and maintain that pertinent Internet data. I now keep that information snugly beside my desktop. I did searches on various Internet bookstores, in search of such a printed book, as I wanted my CPU companion to look better than the ratty, scraggly-edged collection of pages that is my spiral notebook. I try to be careful, but that concoction of tear out pages has soaked up more sodas and glasses of water, than I'd care to acknowledge. The ink has run on most pages. Many pages are missing. It's kind of embarrassing, but I thought to myself that there MUST BE A BETTER WAY. And yet…there is! That is how this book was born.

My prayer is for neater Internet usage wherever users consume various liquids and search desperately for that single password.

Ginae B. McDonald.

Introduction (How to Use This Book)

To take one look at The Internet Companion, the answer to your Internet organization problems may be clearly solved, simply with its purchase, or you may require the apportioned ten minutes.

Still…(Or…for those of you who are not inspired simply with what you see—let us go further).

For those of you of alphabetical leanings—feel free to organize in this manner.

For those of you of a categorical mindset—feel free to organize in this manner.

For those of you who are actively involved with the mixing of fruits, you may find it very satisfying to go crazy and mix within the match. To me, this kind of defeats the purpose of organization, but I am not you, nor are you, me.

Here is a list of recommended divisions:
Animals
Arts
Auctions
Blank
Bookmarks
Chat
Contests
E-Mail

E-Zines
Family
Games
Gardening
Kids
Letters of the Alphabet
Newsgroups
Not For Kids
Rewards
School
Sports
Studies
URL's
Web Design
Writers

Here is a list of recommended web sites:
http://www.KittyKatdc.com
http://www.JustGinae.com

DIVISIONS

_____

Division Name

_____

_____

_____

_____

_____

_____

_____

_____

_____

_____

_____

_____

_____

_____

_____

_____

_____

_____

_____

_____

_____

_____

_____

DIVISIONS

Division Name

_____

_____

_____

_____

_____

_____

_____

_____

_____

_____

_____

_____

_____

_____

_____

_____

_____

_____

_____

_____

_____

_____

_____

_____

_____

_____

DIVISIONS

Division Name

_____

_____

_____

_____

_____

_____

_____

_____

_____

_____

_____

_____

_____

_____

_____

_____

_____

_____

_____

Divisions

<u>Division Name</u>

_____

_____

_____

_____

_____

_____

_____

_____

_____

_____

_____

_____

_____

_____

_____

_____

_____

_____

_____

_____

DIVISIONS

Division Name

_____

_____

_____

_____

_____

_____

_____

_____

_____

_____

_____

_____

_____

_____

_____

_____

_____

_____

_____

_____

DIVISIONS

DIVISIONS

Division Name

_____

_____

_____

_____

_____

_____

_____

_____

_____

_____

_____

_____

_____

_____

_____

_____

_____

_____

_____

_____

_____

DIVISIONS

Division Name

_____

_____

_____

_____

_____

_____

_____

_____

_____

_____

_____

_____

_____

_____

_____

_____

_____

_____

_____

_____

_____

DIVISIONS

Division Name

_____

_____

_____

_____

_____

_____

_____

_____

_____

_____

_____

_____

_____

_____

_____

_____

_____

_____

_____

_____

_____

DIVISIONS

Division Name

_____

_____

_____

_____

_____

_____

_____

_____

_____

_____

_____

_____

_____

_____

_____

_____

_____

_____

_____

_____

DIVISIONS

Division Name

_____

_____

_____

_____

_____

_____

_____

_____

_____

_____

_____

_____

_____

_____

_____

_____

_____

_____

_____

_____

_____

DIVISIONS

Division Name

_____

_____

_____

_____

_____

_____

_____

_____

_____

_____

_____

_____

_____

_____

_____

_____

_____

_____

_____

_____

DIVISIONS

Division Name

_____

_____

_____

_____

_____

_____

_____

_____

_____

_____

_____

_____

_____

_____

_____

_____

_____

_____

_____

_____

_____

DIVISIONS

Division Name

_____

_____

_____

_____

_____

_____

_____

_____

_____

_____

_____

_____

_____

_____

_____

_____

_____

_____

_____

_____

_____

DIVISIONS

Division Name

_____

_____

_____

_____

_____

_____

_____

_____

_____

_____

_____

_____

_____

_____

_____

_____

_____

_____

_____

_____

DIVISIONS

Division Name

_____

_____

_____

_____

_____

_____

_____

_____

_____

_____

_____

_____

_____

_____

_____

_____

_____

_____

_____

_____

_____

DIVISIONS

Division Name

_____

_____

_____

_____

_____

_____

_____

_____

_____

_____

_____

_____

_____

_____

_____

_____

_____

_____

_____

_____

_____

DIVISIONS

<u>   </u>
Division Name

_____

_____

_____

_____

_____

_____

_____

_____

_____

_____

_____

_____

_____

_____

_____

_____

_____

_____

_____

_____

DIVISIONS

Division Name

_____

_____

_____

_____

_____

_____

_____

_____

_____

_____

_____

_____

_____

_____

_____

_____

_____

_____

_____

_____

_____

DIVISIONS

Division Name

_____

_____

_____

_____

_____

_____

_____

_____

_____

_____

_____

_____

_____

_____

_____

_____

_____

_____

_____

_____

_____

DIVISIONS

Division Name

_____

_____

_____

_____

_____

_____

_____

_____

_____

_____

_____

_____

_____

_____

_____

_____

_____

_____

_____

_____

DIVISIONS

_____

Division Name

_____
_____
_____
_____
_____
_____
_____
_____
_____
_____
_____
_____
_____
_____
_____
_____
_____
_____
_____
_____
_____

DIVISIONS

_____

Division Name

_____
_____
_____
_____
_____
_____
_____
_____
_____
_____
_____
_____
_____
_____
_____
_____
_____
_____
_____
_____
_____

DIVISIONS

_____

Division Name

_____
_____
_____
_____
_____
_____
_____
_____
_____
_____
_____
_____
_____
_____
_____
_____
_____
_____
_____

DIVISIONS

Division Name

_____

_____

_____

_____

_____

_____

_____

_____

_____

_____

_____

_____

_____

_____

_____

_____

_____

_____

_____

DIVISIONS

Division Name

_____

_____

_____

_____

_____

_____

_____

_____

_____

_____

_____

_____

_____

_____

_____

_____

_____

_____

_____

_____

DIVISIONS

Division Name

_____

_____

_____

_____

_____

_____

_____

_____

_____

_____

_____

_____

_____

_____

_____

_____

_____

_____

_____

_____

_____

DIVISIONS

Division Name

_____

_____

_____

_____

_____

_____

_____

_____

_____

_____

_____

_____

_____

_____

_____

_____

_____

_____

_____

_____

DIVISIONS

Division Name

_____
_____
_____
_____
_____
_____
_____
_____
_____
_____
_____
_____
_____
_____
_____
_____
_____
_____
_____
_____
_____

DIVISIONS

Division Name

_____

_____

_____

_____

_____

_____

_____

_____

_____

_____

_____

_____

_____

_____

_____

_____

_____

_____

_____

DIVISIONS

<u>Division Name</u>

_____

_____

_____

_____

_____

_____

_____

_____

_____

_____

_____

_____

_____

_____

_____

_____

_____

_____

_____

DIVISIONS

Division Name

_____

_____

_____

_____

_____

_____

_____

_____

_____

_____

_____

_____

_____

_____

_____

_____

_____

_____

_____

_____

_____

DIVISIONS

DIVISIONS

Division Name

DIVISIONS

Division Name

_____

_____

_____

_____

_____

_____

_____

_____

_____

_____

_____

_____

_____

_____

_____

_____

_____

_____

_____

_____

DIVISIONS

<u>Division Name</u>

_____

_____

_____

_____

_____

_____

_____

_____

_____

_____

_____

_____

_____

_____

_____

_____

_____

_____

_____

_____

_____

Divisions

Division Name

_____

_____

_____

_____

_____

_____

_____

_____

_____

_____

_____

_____

_____

_____

_____

_____

_____

_____

_____

_____

_____

DIVISIONS

Division Name

_____

_____

_____

_____

_____

_____

_____

_____

_____

_____

_____

_____

_____

_____

_____

_____

_____

_____

_____

_____

DIVISIONS

Division Name

DIVISIONS

Division Name

DIVISIONS

DIVISIONS

Division Name

_____

_____

_____

_____

_____

_____

_____

_____

_____

_____

_____

_____

_____

_____

_____

_____

_____

_____

_____

_____

_____

_____

Divisions

_____

Division Name

_____
_____
_____
_____
_____
_____
_____
_____
_____
_____
_____
_____
_____
_____
_____
_____
_____
_____
_____
_____
_____
_____

DIVISIONS

Division Name

_____

_____

_____

_____

_____

_____

_____

_____

_____

_____

_____

_____

_____

_____

_____

_____

_____

_____

_____

_____

_____

_____

_____

_____

DIVISIONS

Division Name

_____

_____

_____

_____

_____

_____

_____

_____

_____

_____

_____

_____

_____

_____

_____

_____

_____

_____

_____

_____

_____

DIVISIONS

Division Name

DIVISIONS

Division Name

_____

_____

_____

_____

_____

_____

_____

_____

_____

_____

_____

_____

_____

_____

_____

_____

_____

_____

_____

_____

DIVISIONS

<u>Division Name</u>

_____

_____

_____

_____

_____

_____

_____

_____

_____

_____

_____

_____

_____

_____

_____

_____

_____

_____

_____

_____

DIVISIONS

Division Name

_____

_____

_____

_____

_____

_____

_____

_____

_____

_____

_____

_____

_____

_____

_____

_____

_____

_____

_____

_____

_____

_____

DIVISIONS

Division Name

_____

_____

_____

_____

_____

_____

_____

_____

_____

_____

_____

_____

_____

_____

_____

_____

_____

_____

_____

_____

DIVISIONS

Division Name

_____
_____
_____
_____
_____
_____
_____
_____
_____
_____
_____
_____
_____
_____
_____
_____
_____
_____

DIVISIONS

Division Name

_____

_____

_____

_____

_____

_____

_____

_____

_____

_____

_____

_____

_____

_____

_____

_____

_____

_____

_____

_____

_____

DIVISIONS

Division Name

_____

_____

_____

_____

_____

_____

_____

_____

_____

_____

_____

_____

_____

_____

_____

_____

_____

_____

_____

_____

_____

_____

DIVISIONS

Division Name

DIVISIONS

Division Name

_____

_____

_____

_____

_____

_____

_____

_____

_____

_____

_____

_____

_____

_____

_____

_____

_____

_____

_____

_____

DIVISIONS

Division Name

_____
_____
_____
_____
_____
_____
_____
_____
_____
_____
_____
_____
_____
_____
_____
_____
_____
_____
_____
_____
_____

DIVISIONS

Division Name

_____

_____

_____

_____

_____

_____

_____

_____

_____

_____

_____

_____

_____

_____

_____

_____

_____

_____

_____

DIVISIONS

DIVISIONS

Division Name

_____

_____

_____

_____

_____

_____

_____

_____

_____

_____

_____

_____

_____

_____

_____

_____

_____

_____

_____

_____

_____

DIVISIONS

Division Name

_____

_____

_____

_____

_____

_____

_____

_____

_____

_____

_____

_____

_____

_____

_____

_____

_____

_____

_____

DIVISIONS

Division Name

_____

_____

_____

_____

_____

_____

_____

_____

_____

_____

_____

_____

_____

_____

_____

_____

_____

_____

_____

_____

_____

DIVISIONS

Division Name

_____

_____

_____

_____

_____

_____

_____

_____

_____

_____

_____

_____

_____

_____

_____

_____

_____

_____

_____

_____

_____

Divisions

_____

_____

_____

_____

_____

_____

_____

_____

_____

_____

_____

_____

_____

_____

_____

_____

_____

_____

_____

_____

_____

_____

DIVISIONS

Division Name

_____

_____

_____

_____

_____

_____

_____

_____

_____

_____

_____

_____

_____

_____

_____

_____

_____

_____

_____

_____

DIVISIONS

Division Name

_____

_____

_____

_____

_____

_____

_____

_____

_____

_____

_____

_____

_____

_____

_____

_____

_____

_____

_____

_____

DIVISIONS

Division Name

_____

_____

_____

_____

_____

_____

_____

_____

_____

_____

_____

_____

_____

_____

_____

_____

_____

_____

_____

_____

_____

_____

_____

DIVISIONS

_____

Division Name

_____
_____
_____
_____
_____
_____
_____
_____
_____
_____
_____
_____
_____
_____
_____
_____
_____
_____
_____
_____
_____
_____

DIVISIONS

Division Name

_____

_____

_____

_____

_____

_____

_____

_____

_____

_____

_____

_____

_____

_____

_____

_____

_____

_____

_____

_____

_____

_____

DIVISIONS

Division Name

_____

_____

_____

_____

_____

_____

_____

_____

_____

_____

_____

_____

_____

_____

_____

_____

_____

_____

_____

_____

DIVISIONS

_____

Division Name

_____
_____
_____
_____
_____
_____
_____
_____
_____
_____
_____
_____
_____
_____
_____
_____
_____
_____
_____
_____
_____
_____
_____

APPENDIX

Time Conversion Chart.

Military	PST	MST	CST	EST
00:00	Midnight	1am	2am	3am
01:00	1am	2am	3am	4am
02:00	2am	3am	4am	5am
03:00	3am	4am	5am	6am
04:00	4am	5am	6am	7am
05:00	5am	6am	7am	8am
06:00	6am	7am	8am	9am
07:00	7am	8am	9am	10am
08:00	8am	9am	10am	11am
09:00	9am	10am	11am	12noon
10:00	10am	11am	12noon	1pm
11:00	11am	12noon	1pm	2pm
12:00	12noon	1pm	2pm	3pm
13:00	1pm	2pm	3pm	4pm
14:00	2pm	3pm	4pm	5pm
15:00	3pm	4pm	5pm	6pm
16:00	4pm	5pm	6pm	7pm
17:00	5pm	6pm	7pm	8pm
18:00	6pm	7pm	8pm	9pm
19:00	7pm	8pm	9pm	10pm
20:00	8pm	9pm	10pm	11pm
21:00	9pm	10pm	11pm	12midnight
22:00	10pm	11pm	12midnight	1am
23:00	11pm	12midnight	1am	2am

.

0-595-21428-2

www.ingramcontent.com/pod-product-compliance
Lightning Source LLC
Chambersburg PA
CBHW051254050326
40689CB00007B/1192